THE ART OF MINDFULNESS

MINDFUL WRITING

BY STEPHANIE FINNE

BLUE OWL
BOOKS

TIPS FOR CAREGIVERS

Social and emotional learning (SEL) helps children manage emotions, create and achieve goals, maintain relationships, learn how to feel empathy, and make good decisions. The SEL approach will help children establish positive habits in communication, cooperation, and decision-making. By incorporating SEL in early reading, children will be better equipped to build confidence and foster positive peer networks.

BEFORE READING

Talk to the reader about what he or she likes to write.

Discuss: Do you like writing? Do you enjoy journaling or writing letters, stories, or poems? What do you like about it?

AFTER READING

Discuss how the reader can write mindfully.

Discuss: How can you include writing in your daily routine? Where can you go to write privately about your emotions?

SEL GOAL

Some students may struggle to express their emotions, making it hard to regulate their thoughts and behaviors. Help readers develop these skills by learning to tune into their minds and put their thoughts on paper. Mindful writing can help readers slow down, focus, and reflect on their feelings.

TABLE OF CONTENTS

CHAPTER 1

WHY WRITE?

Mindfulness means paying attention to our **emotions**. It also means being in the present moment. Writing is one way to be mindful.

Writing helps us put words to our thoughts. It helps us **focus** on what is happening right now. It can also help us make sense of what is happening around us.

There are many ways to write mindfully. Writing poetry can help you **express** emotions. Journaling helps you examine your emotions. Writing **fiction** helps you practice **creativity**. Writing thank-you letters helps you practice **gratitude**.

PRIVATE WRITING

It isn't always easy to talk about feelings. Writing gives you another option! Journaling, poetry, and story-writing are private ways to explore your thoughts and feelings.

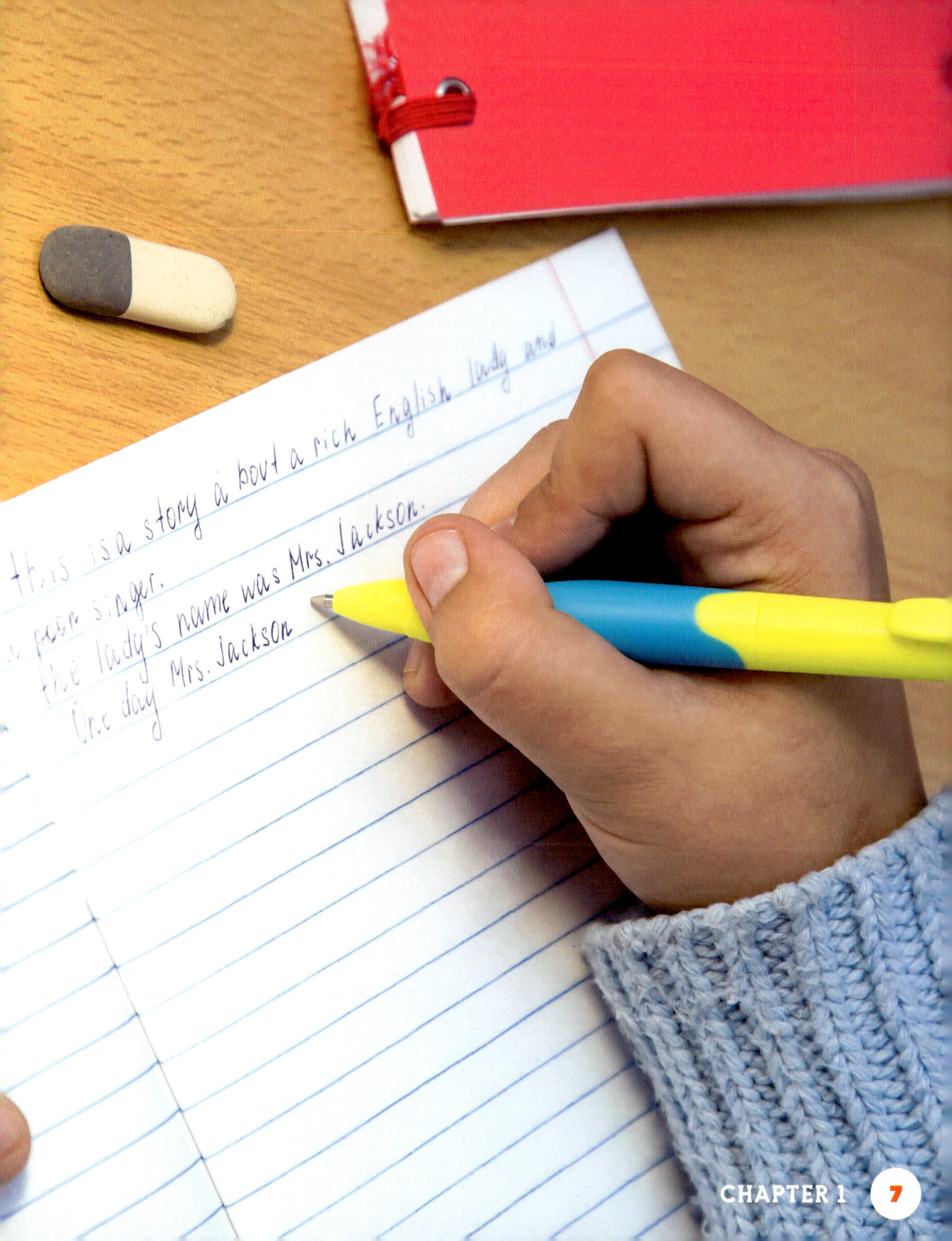
this is a story a bout a rich English lady and
a poor singer.
the lady's name was Mrs. Jackson.
One day Mrs. Jackson

CHAPTER 2

LET'S WRITE!

You don't need fancy tools or perfect spelling to write. All you need is something to write with and something to write on.

A journal is a great writing tool. You can carry it with you or leave it at home. It can help you set an **intention** to write every day. Use your journal to write about anything you want.

HELPFUL HINT: Try to write at the same time each day. This will help you form a **habit** of writing.

Journaling is one way to **reflect** on your day or an event. It can help you organize your thoughts and emotions.

Step 1: Gather your journal and what you like to write with. Find a private space where you feel comfortable.

Step 2: Then start writing! What are you thinking about today? Did something happen that made you happy, sad, or confused? Write about what happened. How did your mind and body feel?

THANKFUL WRITING

Gratitude journaling is writing about things that make you happy. Try it! Each week, write down three things you are grateful for.

You can write your thoughts, feelings, or ideas about nature in a nature journal.

Step 1: Use a regular notebook or staple pieces of paper together to create a journal. Find a safe, comfortable place to **observe** nature.

Step 2: Tune into your senses. What do you see, hear, and smell? Write about these things.

Step 3: What can you feel? Are there fallen leaves or flowers for you to examine? Write about what they look like. Draw them if you like! You can even decorate your pages with them.

nature journal

The leaves are starting to change color. I see brown, red, orange, and yellow leaves.

acorns are falling from trees

HELPFUL HINT: Short phrases and labels count as writing. They can help you remember the details of what you saw in nature.

Writing poetry is another way to express your feelings. Poems don't need to rhyme, but they should make you feel something when you read them.

First, think of a topic. How does it make you feel? Write a list of words that describe your topic.

SENSORY WRITING

Use your senses to think of words for what you see, hear, smell, touch, or taste.

Then start writing!

Step 1: Begin your poem with a statement or a question about your topic. Use the words from your list to describe it.

Step 2: Use line breaks to show a reader when to pause. This gives your poem **rhythm**. Line breaks can also help you rhyme if you want to.

Step 3: Reread your writing. Practice reading it out loud. How do the words sound together? Can you add more description? Take out phrases that don't feel right.

HELPFUL HINT: What is your topic? Use that to create a title for your poem.

My Pet Dog

My pet dog is white and black.
My pet dog likes it when I scratch his back.

I feel happy when I take my pet dog for a walk.
I wish that my pet dog could talk!

CHAPTER 3

READING YOUR WRITING

Rereading your writing can help remind you of the past. It can show you how you have grown and changed. It can remind you how you've dealt with difficult situations.

Do not **judge** your spelling or handwriting. Focus on how writing helped your mind and body.

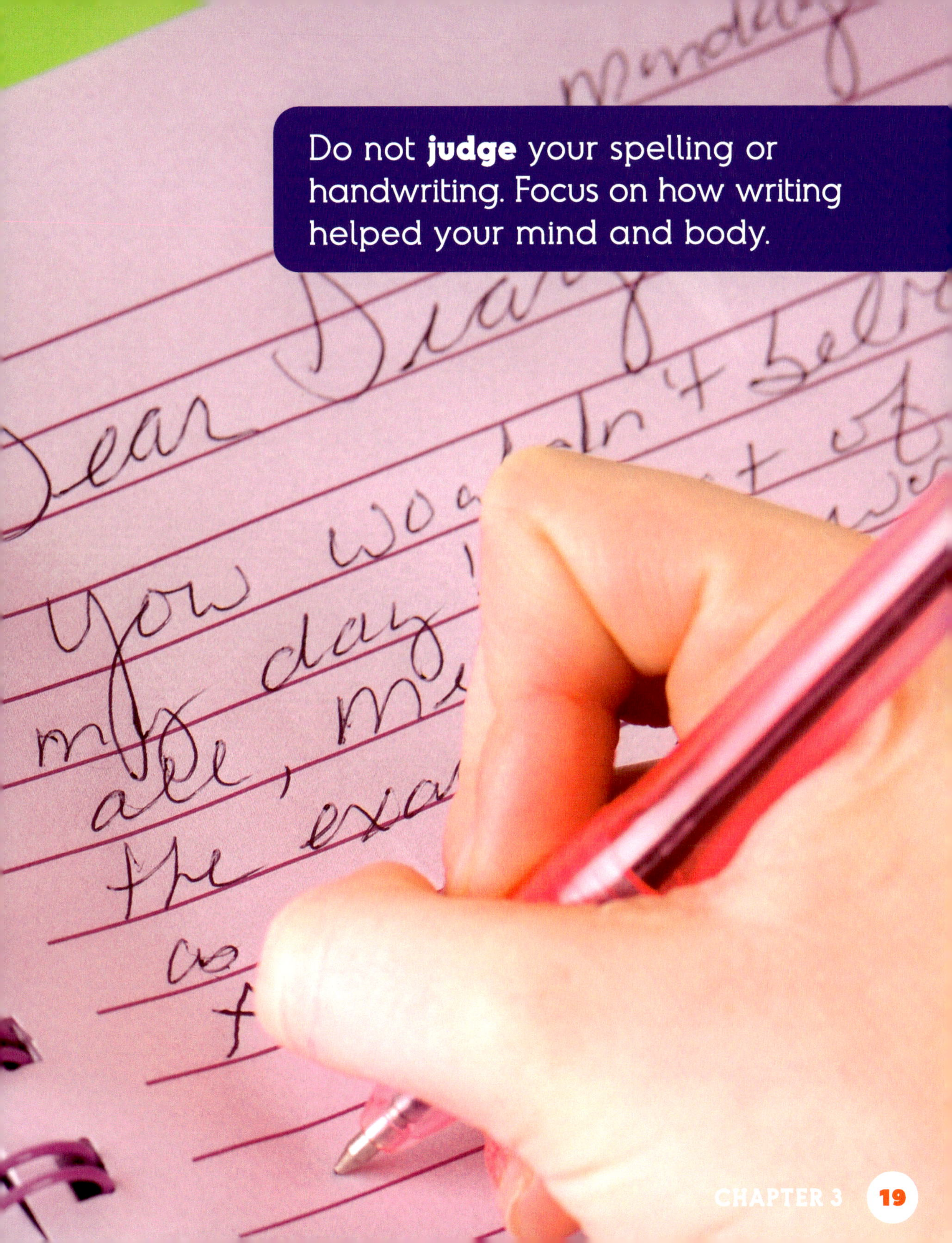

The **process** of writing is the important part. Writing helps you focus and be in the present moment. It can help you name what you are feeling.

After you write, check in with your mind and body. How does writing make you feel?

GOALS AND TOOLS

GROW WITH GOALS

Writing mindfully can help you stay in the moment.
Try these things:

Goal: Think about an event or something that has happened to you. Write about it.

Goal: Pay attention to how your breathing changes as you write.

Goal: Look at what you have written without judgment. Everything you create is special. Pick out at least three things you like about what you wrote or how you wrote it.

TRY THIS!

A gratitude journal helps you reflect on your day and your relationships.

1. Think about what made you feel happy today. If you need ideas, answer these questions:
    - What made you smile today?
    - Who did something kind for you today?
    - Who made you feel loved today?
2. Write down why those things made you feel happy and why you are grateful for them. Write as much or as little as you like.
3. Each day, reread the entry from the previous day. Then add a new entry.

GLOSSARY

creativity
The ability to make new things or think of new ideas.

emotions
Feelings, such as happiness, sadness, or anger.

express
To show what you feel or think with words, writing, or actions.

fiction
Something that is made up.

focus
To concentrate on something.

gratitude
A feeling of being grateful or thankful.

habit
An activity or behavior that you do regularly, often without thinking about it.

intention
Something you mean to do.

judge
To form an opinion about something or someone.

mindfulness
A mentality achieved by focusing on the present moment and calmly recognizing and accepting your feelings, thoughts, and sensations.

observe
To watch someone or something closely, especially to learn something.

process
A series of actions or steps that create something.

reflect
To think carefully or seriously about something.

rhythm
A repeated pattern of sound or movement in music, dance, or poetry.

TO LEARN MORE

FACT SURFER

Finding more information is as easy as 1, 2, 3.

1. Go to www.factsurfer.com
2. Enter "**mindfulwriting**" into the search box.
3. Choose your book to see a list of websites.

INDEX

Blue Owl Books are published by Jump!, 5357 Penn Avenue South, Minneapolis, MN 55419, www.jumplibrary.com

Library of Congress Cataloging-in-Publication Data

Names: Finne, Stephanie, author.
Title: Mindful writing / Stephanie Finne.
Description: Minneapolis, MN: Jump!, Inc., [2022]
Series: The art of mindfulness | Includes index. | Audience: Ages 7–10
Identifiers: LCCN 2021035639 (print)
LCCN 2021035640 (ebook)
ISBN 9781636903675 (hardcover)
ISBN 9781636903682 (paperback)
ISBN 9781636903699 (ebook)
Subjects: LCSH: Authorship–Juvenile literature. | Mindfulness (Psychology)–Juvenile literature.
Classification: LCC PN159 .F55 2022 (print) | LCC PN159 (ebook) | DDC 808.02–dc23
LC record available at https://lccn.loc.gov/2021035639
LC ebook record available at https://lccn.loc.gov/2021035640

Editor: Jenna Gleisner
Designer: Michelle Sonnek

Photo Credits: sashahaltam/Shutterstock, cover; Littlekidmonent/Shutterstock, 1; Vitalina Rybakova/Shutterstock, 3; Africa Studio/Shutterstock, 4; LightField Studios/Shutterstock, 5; Andrey Safonov/Shutterstock, 6–7; Hemarat Studio/Shutterstock, 8; Odua Images/Shutterstock, 9; Studio Romantic/Shutterstock, 10–11; Aleksandrs Samuilovs/Shutterstock, 12–13, 16–17; Iryna Mylinska/Shutterstock, 14–15; Kozlik/Shutterstock, 18; Cheryl Casey/Shutterstock, 19; Inna Vlasova/Shutterstock, 20–21.

Printed in the United States of America at Corporate Graphics in North Mankato, Minnesota.